Palimpsest
Clive Birnie

VERVE
POETRY PRESS
BIRMINGHAM

PUBLISHED BY VERVE POETRY PRESS
https://vervepoetrypress.com
mail@vervepoetrypress.com

FIRST PUBLISHED JAN 2020

Printed and bound in the UK
by Positive Print, Birmingham

ISBN: 978-1-912565-32-0

*for all who stand against
tyranny*

Palimpsest

Imperfections in wood,
natural cracks, rings,
even tree bark,
carefully rendered into
styling elements by a woman who
could smell the sea coming,
who could predict the precise second
that red sand rain would arrive
from distant deserts.

The New York Times called
her the perfect dreamy iteration
of a surprising discovery, but
her own research said tricks
of the light
                (fraudulent
presentations may indicate
otherwise) when the going is soft
(good-to-soft in places)
Nantwich, Penzance, Sheffield,

chances are,
these days, if you want to
find exactly the right thing,
your breathless pleas
for help will
be on tonight's evening news.

She got herself a job as a chamber-maid,
went from room to room rifling
though guests' possessions, trying
on their perfumes, stealing their shoes,
their luggage, an *Aston Martin* and a villa
on the Riviera. A vast slag heal of junk and
ephemera distorting her sense of self.

Palimpsest has an irregular history.
Hints of a relationship. Knows English, Latin,
learning Mandarin in New York. Born 14 May 1984.
Likes coke. Likes money. Likes poking around
other people's stolen memories.

She can perfectly measure elapsed time,
it is said, perfectly measure the
descending scale of a life with a
simple press of a finger on lips.

Flipping telepathic triggers, an assassin of convention,
she likes AK47s, red *Gucci* boots, short skirts
and adventure.

It began around sundown, a couple of city slickers
in the desert. Stranded. A lonely canyon.
Fire. Herbicides. Yellow skin-burning chemicals.

"Look, it could happen to anyone," Palimpsest said,
and spat to show her disgust. "Pigweed, dogbane,
sow thistle, stink grass. My secret medicine, but
it didn't help 'em none. It's experimental evolution.
I eke out a living in the harshest regions of the world.
Put it this way, they ain't retiring to Florida anytime soon."

Palimpsest had a history of addiction.
To whisky, prescription drugs and wedding
cake. There were false starts of course, one fiancé
took an overdose and another drowned. They say
her first husband, a schizophrenic, blew his brains
out after they parted. In rapid succession she married
a sailor, an albino piano tuner, Elvis Presley
(he said he was Elvis Presley). "I like to shop around
for a rare deviation, an uncommon variation
from the regular guy. I like a man with no body parts
small enough for me to get my hands around –
and I have pretty damned big hands."

Palimpsest dreams of Robo-Squid
when she wears her *Neuro Mindwave* headset.
Modelled on a 1974 design by engineer Stig Carlsson,
Palimpsest says, "It's comfy but the screen is on the
back of my head – I had to get a friend to change the
Aquabeat to *Splash Dance – Aqua Disco*."

She's an alt-geneticist bio-hacker recharging complex
systems. Her experimental robot dolphin close to
revolution. A smart looking metallic tube more
than ten feet long. A homing chip enabled to
determine the unexpected. It's smarter, more

dangerous and more musical than you might think.
Firefly luminescent but bioengineered, to pump
out sub-aquatic opera at 22,000 feet.

If you believe the rumours Palimpsest
keeps a million dead creatures in the art
quarantine facility, which is plausible for sure.

Every specimen died in her arms, they say.
"I feel very vulnerable," the curator likes to whine.
To prove the point, he shows
a skinned, mummified rabbit half eaten
by the dreaded Guernsey carpet beetle.

His ubiquitous hard sell is starting to grate.
Kill pests are uploaded to museums in the UK
but the digital forensics are ambiguous, her DNA
unmapped. Fingerprints missing from the database.
She keeps off the mainframes, deals behind
doors, a secretive breeder of ghost cats.

Every object that met the eye was unfamiliar but beautiful.

Palimpsest hacking something in the bathroom,
the floor covered in the spread of half finished jigsaw.

She sat and watched him wolfing.

Suddenly a dark flash swam through his arc of light
larger than any normal fish.

The blood flooding across, soaking the house.
She went into the black, waded in to search,
went into the river and bent down to squint
for any left behind, bobbing in the water.

They were close now.

I have dragged my lazy self out of hibernation
to this year's *Strategic Yoga Festival*. You can call me
apathetic, you can call me hipster, but you know
where that ends. North Shore's *Turtle Bay Resort*. A few
hundred lonely souls who think a couple days of
appropriation will wash away their sins.

This is no hippie fest, nor teeming with pretension.
With a nearly naked soccer-mom, a dreadlocked legal student.
This is morphine. Do you need an infographic? Everyone here
is twenty-nine. Stick-thin. Gymnastic. But listen, without this

I would not be the same person. I'd be somebody else.
Somebody you would not want to meet.

It matters not to me what people think.
Give me instinct. Thought is over rated.

Maybe nobody else would care a lick, but that last answer
is the bottom line, the one reason I keep wheelbarrows
and distressed birdcages and flower frogs all waiting
for a ride home. There's the chorus. There's the black
house barn-siding and stacks of old pots.

What is it that you people want?

Hyper-hip *505 Meats* in
San Francisco serves crunchy
Chicarrones-Vancouver-Dog
sprinkled with black sesame seeds...
but a French version.
I had a local guy who
introduced himself as Floppy.
Dangerously handsome. Scorching.
Highly recommended.
In the region of Palafrugell,
50km from Girona.
Worth it. No-frills.
Came straight off the boat a stone's
throw from our table...

                                    sizzling.

Seriously – did you see the
clothes on celebrity lover-boy's
stylist?

I had three weeks disguised like
Rita Hayworth in Havana.

Look, I knew the kids would all
be in bikinis, so I tried
dressing up, but have you seen
the collections?

I watch films for inspiration & rob
vintage shops, stand in the street
singing, all queen of tweed
& mismatched sneakers
to cover the blackfoot,

but it does me no good.

Old people don't scare Palimpsest,
what she calls granny-grunge comprises
cream short cashmere cardigans
& grosgrain ribbon all sewn up.

That's reality youth diluting,
only sophisticate starlets may stop
spiralling into bad karma,
but at her age, so what?

Certainly *Charlotte Street Hot
Darjeeling* was first bill
for the time of year
- in concentrated capsules -
but cool, rather cloudy at times,
becoming
variable
later,
in the south.

Palimpsest was a member of the Big Sur
Gun Club. For me, it went beyond the initial
intrigue. God knows she had form modelling
expectation and the chestnut hair would not
have struck her as a downside.

"All in all I'm not displeased,"
she said. "It eliminates doubt. I began
to hunt for someone nerdy,
and I love him. End of. 80% Hollywood.
Accept it was hard for me to do, because
I just wanted to lose myself in the bubble
world of being Palimpsest."

I'm told the woman doesn't
fuck around when you're not her cup of tea.
Singing, because she has that Elvis voice,
"I'm the one to blame."

Do you get it? Billy's lost his mind for sure,
now that it's over. The Feds? If there is a case
they ain't gonna pursue it.

You know I heard she let him
choose
the island
outfits
from their
Pacific segue
as a keepsake,
I guess that's progress
of
a
kind.

He stood seven nights at the thresh of the village until
he had darkened and Palimpsest permitted him in.

She stood six cockerels
at the points of a hexagram, circled him five times,
calling to the mountain, to the stream. She assured
me that this fourth time would be final. Tattooed
the spell on his torso with a blackened silver blade.

She cut three feathers from a cormorant's wing. Cored
marrow from its bones. Simmered a thin saffron sauce
laced with pufferfish blood.
She cut a jellyfish in two.
Murmured over and over that he was cleansed of the past,
but not forgiven.
A single red kite stood on the air.
A wild cat twitched in the grass.
The revenant's firstborn stood dressed in red. A cracked
mask of white mud, charcoal black eyes. Palimpsest dug
a shallow grave in the peat. Set some turfs burning. Added
the stones, the cocks, the jellyfish, the cat, the cormorant's
wing and the dead-man's tongue, and we buried him back
in the ground where he belongs.

In Franz Josef land, the melting ice; the glacial retreat.

Leopards adapt to living in cities, so adept
that we do not know they are at hand.

Remnants of a failed utopia. Disused machines,
abandoned buildings, the overreach of technology.

*

Out of ghost lands walk nations haunted by history.

Pay attention.

Sea Wolves beach-combing Canadian islands,
eating whatever the ocean serves up.

Urban civilisation can feel very far away.

*

Welcome to the world.

Be square
and divide
cut the problem small

take shortcuts wherever possible.

Death doesn't mean good-bye.

The nuclear tourist
returns to life

finds beauty
in abstraction.

Cutting pacemakers out of corpses, grinding
bones by hand, Palimpsest doesn't care
to keep her inner existential under wraps.

"Bodies are museums in themselves," she says,
"organ, fat and bone space where we archive,
store and hoard. This capsule (she taps her chest)
I have inscribed with all the learnings of my mouth."

She drinks cerveza-negra con *Colombiana* with
aquadiente shots. Travels the world but holed up
in Santa Cruz. She keeps a number of unrecorded vials
in a hazard-taped cardboard box. With the FBI tight
behind her, word began to spread about her cool
hobby and her brand of alt-repute.

                                      "I am a verb," she says.
"for the defiance you should expect from everyone,
you underestimate, marginalise or disrespect."

She smokes. White dress. Weekend nostrils.
Tattoo-tired-muscles mating
on the back of her neck.

Cold water. Stage shadows. An orange play of light.

A cigarette glows in the night.
That white dress. A back-lit silhouette.
It's all hot air on the rocks. You get a whiff and you're
eager mad fire. High road 100 degrees.

Ship blasts. Fog horns. A mess of blue
lights, there were people out trying to get a look.
                    "I felt very calm, very pure."
She was captured by fluke,
                    a rare patrol car, taken
to the *Gestalt* HQ in that notorious Rue...

"I don't know how I didn't talk.
I just kept saying I knew nothing, that
I had killed to revenge a dead boyfriend,"
                                        They
had decided to shoot her veins out,
to pack her with an anthology of drugs,
to choke her with sensory destruction.
No right-minded person is going to come back
from a gig like that
                    but Palimpsest is,
                    of course, an island bordered by the black
                            waters of an ocean. It comes
as no surprise that she left the facilities
                    looking superb: whether windsurfing
                            or scuba diving, the choice is yours.

I started
getting
mad. And
getting mad
made me
forget about
everything
going on
around me.

You have to
ingratiate
yourself
with people
and then
sometimes
you have to
betray them.

There was
even a goon
patrol to
check no
one had
escaped.

She could have
struck gold.

She might have struck out,

but she's walking away

and
Hollywood
is burning.

You can work the math.

And now,
the final push.

You got
Robo-submission.

Entertain me,

while this
machine

triggers
idiots.

"...and the man who had been favoured with grace," she said.
"As he grew up, his delusions became more specific but
I know a cure for that. Living in the favelas selling street
food as a cover. In these glory days of social media, anyone
with a skillet and an *iPad* can challenge the power of haute cuisine."

She's become an underground guru, an elusive philosopher.
"It would be elitist if I closed a velvet rope and only let
in certain people. I seek to eliminate rank, to equalise criteria...

start-ups democratising
process...
                    there are some
production studios on it...

much investor attention...

and then to monetise... we haven't

                but...

this has to support itself...

it could be a lot like *Craigslist.*"

Evolution.
The Moon landings.
Fake vaccinations.
Wax.

Polyester.
Fumed silicate.
Genetically modified carbon black.

Protein.
Biology.
Astronomy.
DNA.

Confluence gastronomy.
Shadow titan machines.
Killer idea privacy.
AI baby magazine.

Spot the artist algorithm.
Helping out Big Brother noise.

How to kill deep state government?
Who needs books when photo-year.

Making satellites time cynicism.
You can airport, but beware.

NOTES & ACKNOWLEDGEMENTS

A visual art treatment of *Imperfections in wood* was first published in *Verse Kraken 2* edited by Claire Trévien & Tori Truslow.

Treatments of *She got a job as a chambermaid, Seriously did you see* and *Palimpsest was a member of the Big Sur Gun Club* were published online by *M58*.

A visual art treatment of *Palimpsest dreams of Robo Squid* was published as *Suzannah Dreams of Robo Squid in Aquanauts* edited by Jon Stone and Kirsten Irving, Sidekick Books 2017 and should be credited *after Suzannah Evans.*

Every object that met the eye is my version of a writing exercise from *Aquanauts* completed using random lines from randomly selected pages from *Fen* by Daisy Johnson, Jonathan Cape 2016.

In Franz Josef Land was inspired by conversations with Kate Fox and is a cut up of headlines from *National Geographic* magazine.

The Nuclear Tourist was included in the Evolver Prize 2017 Exhibition at the Thelma Hulbert Gallery.

Colombiana in *Cutting pacemakers out of corpses* is an Irn-Bru like soft drink from Colombia, *Aguadiente* is an anise flavoured spirit and the national drink of Colombia.

Gestalt HQ in *Ship blasts. Fog horns* is a reference to the *Ack-Ack Macaque* novels by award winning British Science Fiction author Gareth L Powell.

According to Voodoo legends pufferfish blood (as mentioned in *He stood seven nights*) is said to contain a powerful neurotoxin and is claimed in some sources to be linked to the creation of Zombies.

Most of the poems included here use text appropriated from a variety of sources, collaged, erased, redacted, cut up and overlaid with original lines to create palimpsests, hence the title of the sequence and the name of the protagonist. Sources include *the Economist, the Financial Times, the Guardian, the Daily Telegraph, Wired, The Week, National Geographic* and *Carmel Magazine* plus other random newspapers, magazines, junk and ephemera collected in waiting rooms, cafes and airports around the world.

ABOUT THE AUTHOR

Clive Birnie is a poet-artist-printmaker who works in both text and visual media. He finds inspiration at a place where poetry and art collide into something which gets called text-based-art but sometimes he types up the results as text only poems such as those included here. He was the *Hashtag#* poet in residence at the StAnza International Poetry Festival in 2016. He has exhibited work at the Saatchi backed The Other Art Fair, the Evolver Prize Exhibition, the Royal West of England Academy Open, Spike Island (during Paul Hawkins's Poem Brut event), the Clifton branch of cafe chain Boston Tea Party and in the public space of Millennium Square, Bristol. *Palimpsest* is the eighth in a sequence of experimental collage and/or visual poetry sequences following *Terminal Insemination Art* (Silkworms Ink 2011), *Cutting Up the Economist* (Burning Eye 2014), *Hashtag# Poetry* (Burning Eye 2016), *O-Neg Alphabet*, a visual response to *Ursprungsalphabet* by Nora Gomringer (Instagram & YouTube 2016), *Impossible Poems* (a self-published limited edition box-set of Polaroid-poems 2017), the *Skye Numbers* series (exhibited at the Other Art Fair Bristol 2017) and *the Lemon Squeezer* (in Bristol, edited by Paul Hawkins, Dostoyevsky Wannabe 2018).

ABOUT VERVE POETRY PRESS

Verve Poetry Press is a fairly new and already award-winning press focussing intently on meeting a need in Birmingham - a need for the vibrant poetry scene here in Brum to find a way to present itself to the poetry world via publication. Co-founded by Stuart Bartholomew and Amerah Saleh, it is publishing poets from all corners of the city - poets that represent the city's varied and energetic qualities and will communicate its many poetic stories.

Added to this is a colourful pamphlet series featuring poets who have previously performed at our sister festival - and a poetry show series which captures the magic of longer poetry performance pieces by poets such as Polarbear and Matt Abbott.

Like the festival, we will strive to think about poetry in inclusive ways and embrace the multiplicity of approaches towards this glorious art.

In 2019 the press was voted Most Innovative Publisher at the Saboteur Awards, and won the Publisher's Award for Poetry Pamphlets at the Michael Marks Awards.

www.vervepoetrypress.com
@VervePoetryPres
mail@vervepoetrypress.com